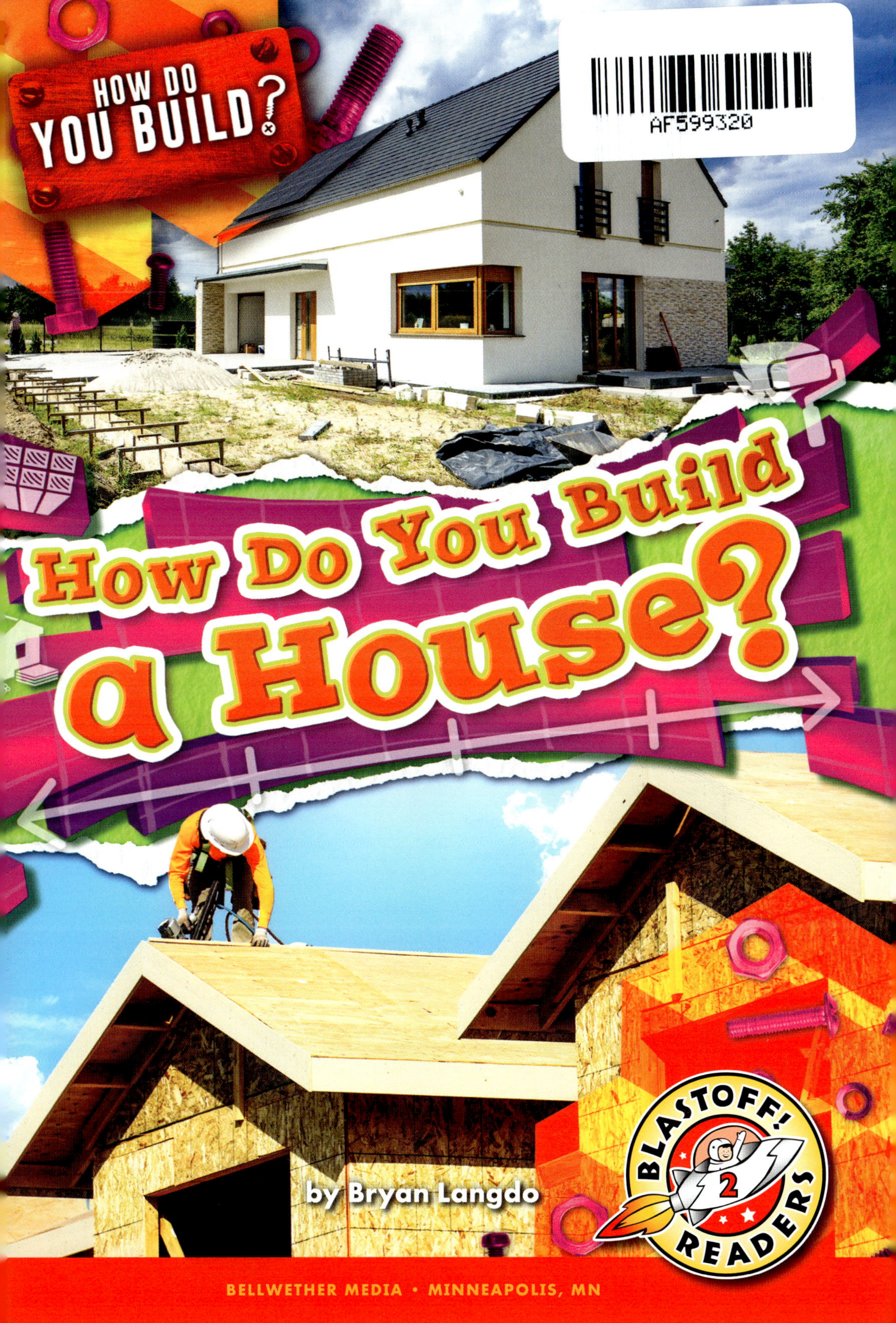
HOW DO
YOU BUILD?
AF599320
How Do You Build
a House?
by Bryan Langdo
BLASTOFF!
2
READERS
BELLWETHER MEDIA • MINNEAPOLIS, MN

Blastoff! Readers are carefully developed by literacy experts to build reading stamina and move students toward fluency by combining standards-based content with developmentally appropriate text.

Level 1 provides the most support through repetition of high-frequency words, light text, predictable sentence patterns, and strong visual support.

Level 2 offers early readers a bit more challenge through varied sentences, increased text load, and text-supportive special features.

Level 3 advances early-fluent readers toward fluency through increased text load, less reliance on photos, advancing concepts, longer sentences, and more complex special features.

★ **Blastoff! Universe**

Reading Level

Grade K

Grades 1–3

Grade 4

This edition first published in 2026 by Bellwether Media, Inc.

Library of Congress Cataloging-in-Publication Data

LC record for How Do You Build a House? available at: https://lccn.loc.gov/2025010708

Editor: Rachael Barnes Book Designer: Josh Brink

Printed in the United States of America, North Mankato, MN.

Table of Contents

A New House 4
Start with Plans 6
Time to Build 8
Home 20
Glossary 22
To Learn More 23
Index 24

A New House

A moving truck arrives. Workers carry boxes and furniture.

A family moves into their new house today!

Start with Plans

A house starts with an **architect**. The architect draws plans.

The plans show what the house will look like. They are also used to get building **permits**.

Time to Build

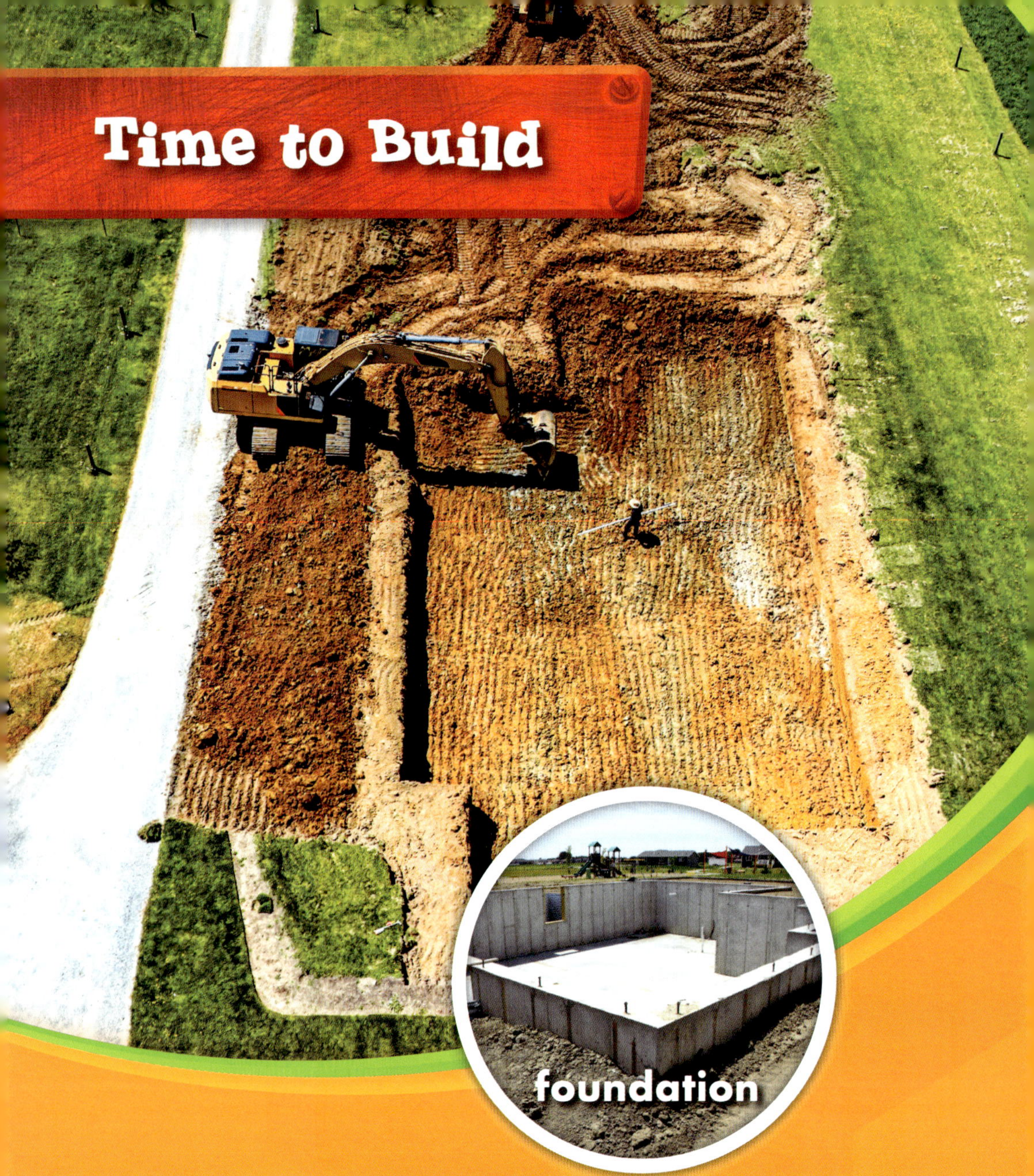

foundation

Workers use machines to clear and flatten the land. Then they build a **foundation**.

Workers often build foundations by pouring **concrete**. Sometimes the foundation includes a basement.

What Do You Need?

concrete

wood

wires

pipes

insulation

drywall

paint

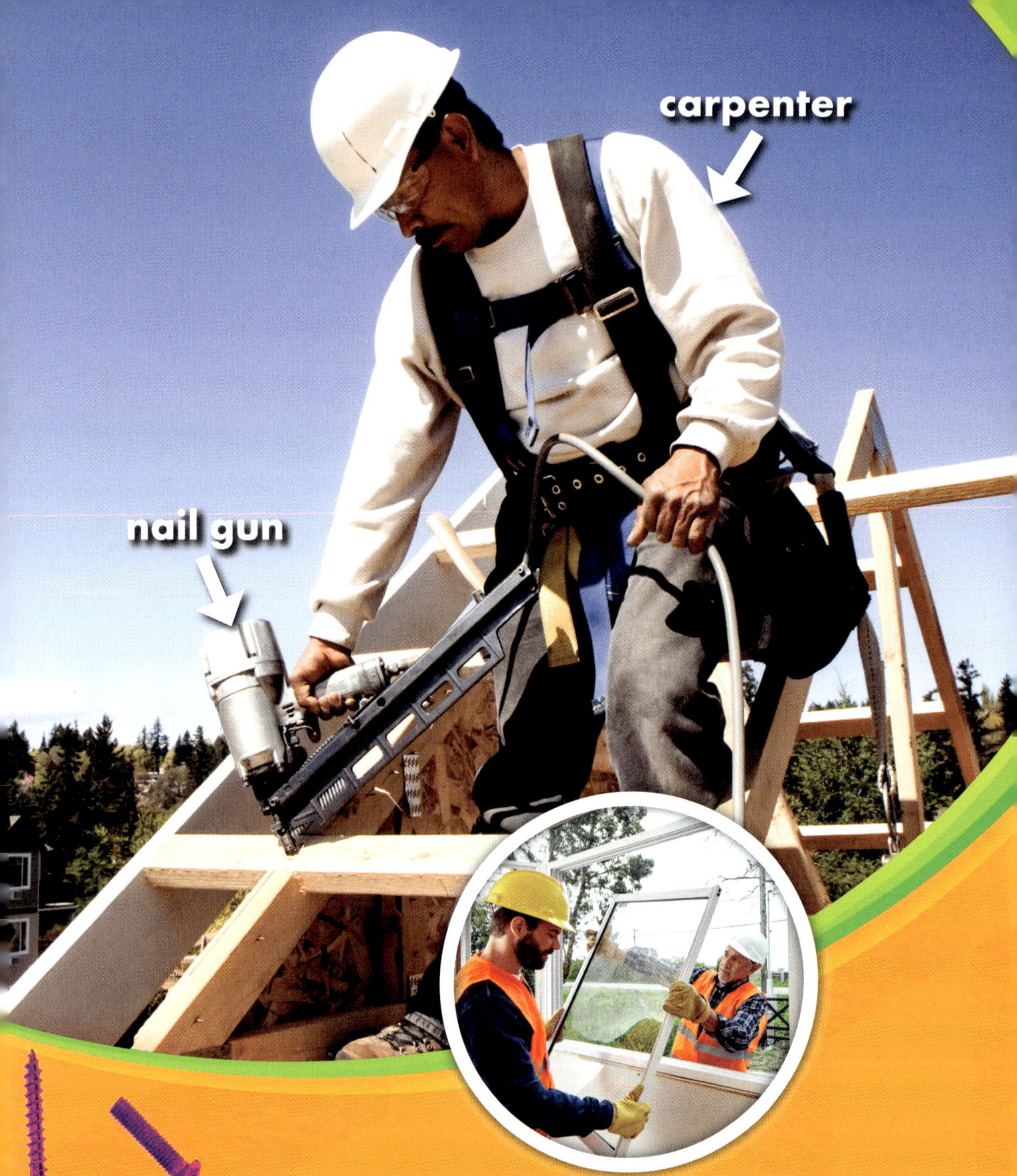

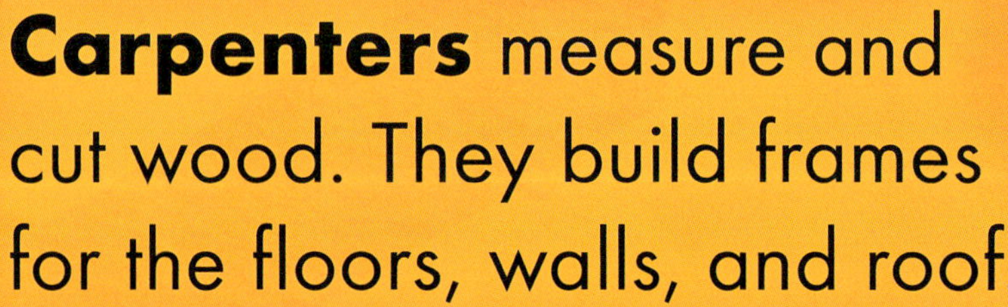

Carpenters measure and cut wood. They build frames for the floors, walls, and roof.

Nail guns help workers build faster! Then workers **install** windows and doors.

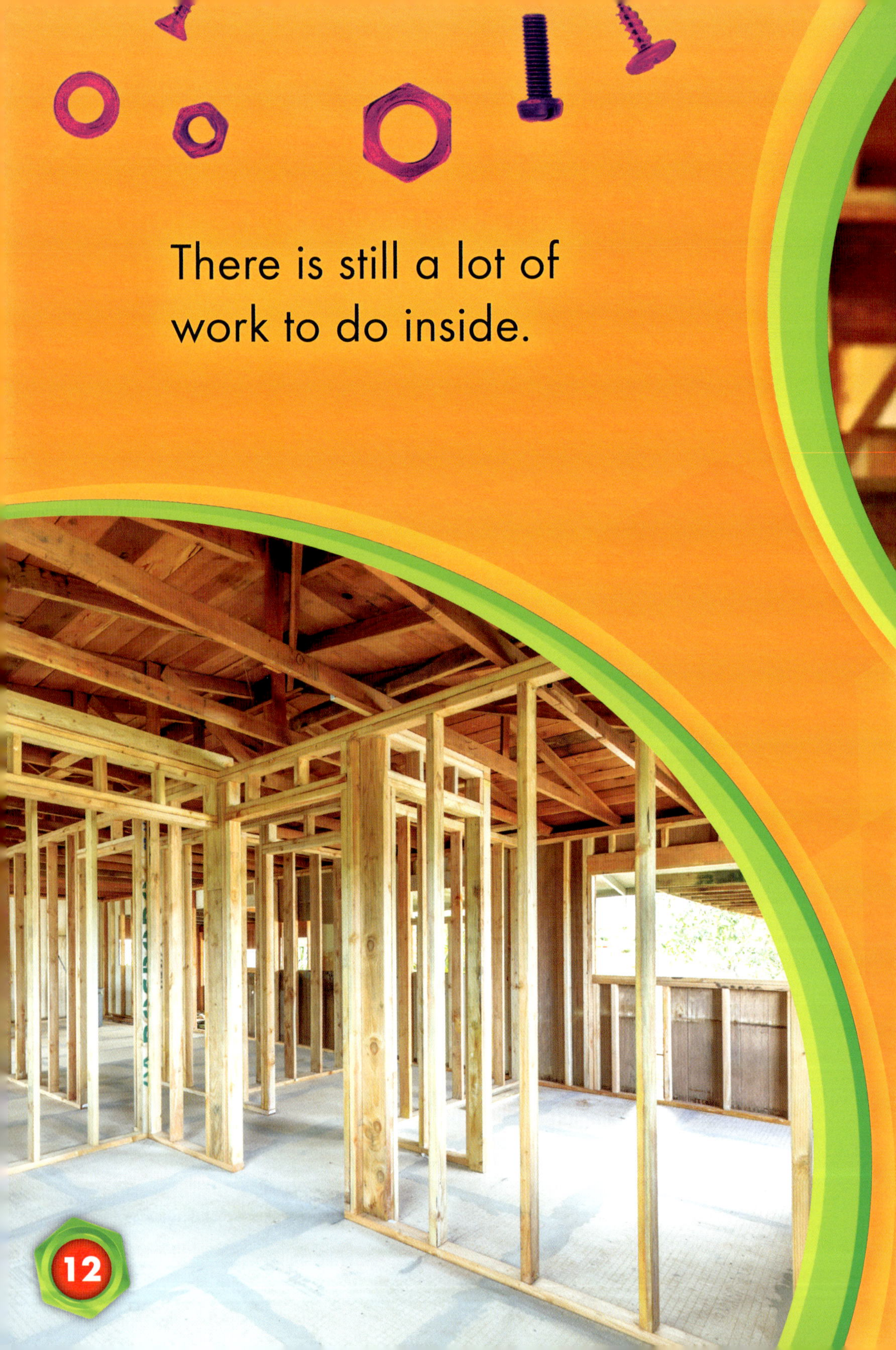

There is still a lot of work to do inside.

plumber

Plumbers fit pipes together. Water will flow through them.

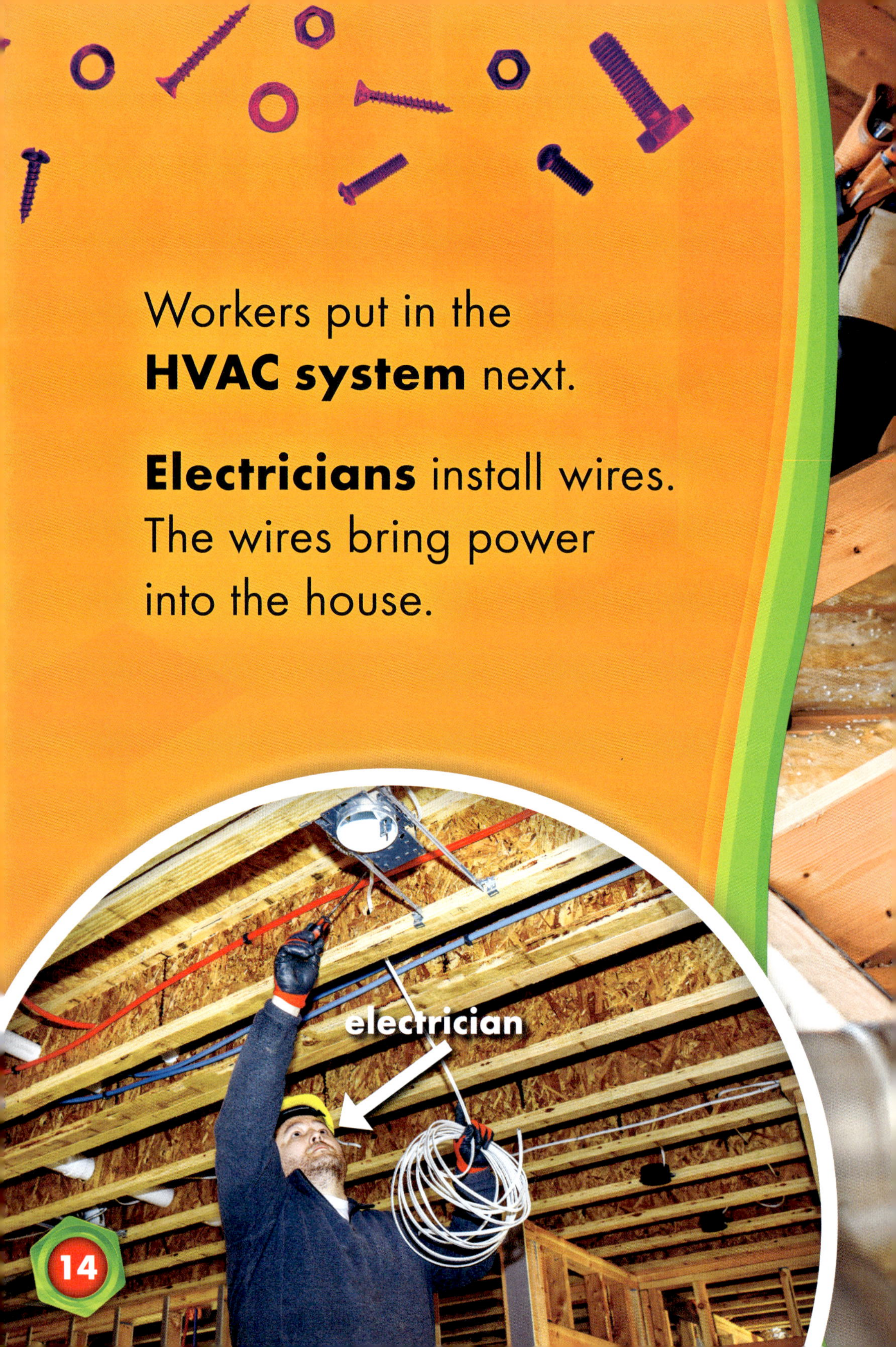

Workers put in the **HVAC system** next.

Electricians install wires. The wires bring power into the house.

HVAC parts

insulation

faucet

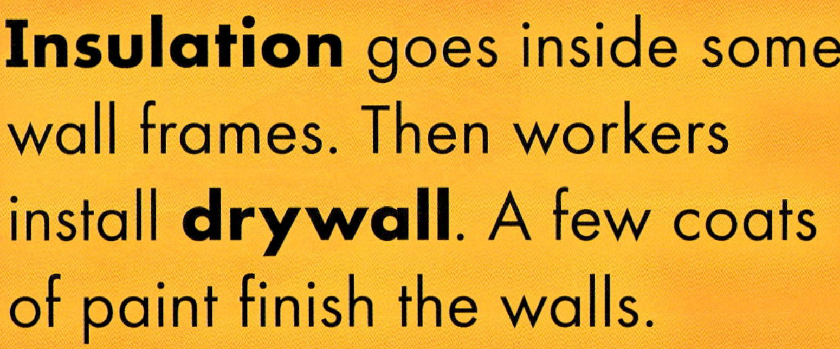

Insulation goes inside some wall frames. Then workers install **drywall**. A few coats of paint finish the walls.

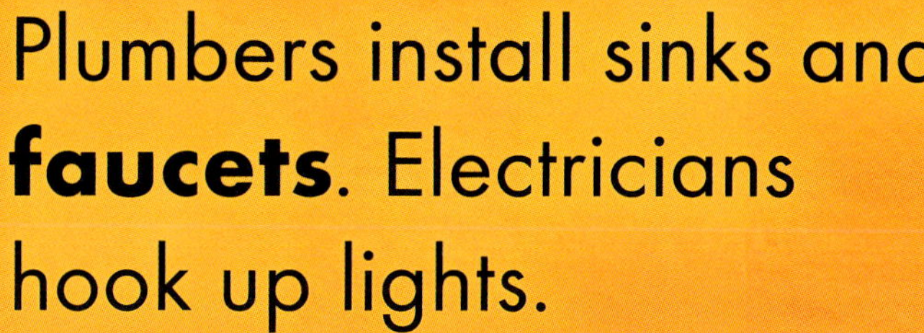

Plumbers install sinks and **faucets**. Electricians hook up lights.

Fallingwater

Location Mill Run, Pennsylvania

Year completed 1938

Size 9,300 square feet (864 square meters)

Famous for a house that is built over a waterfall

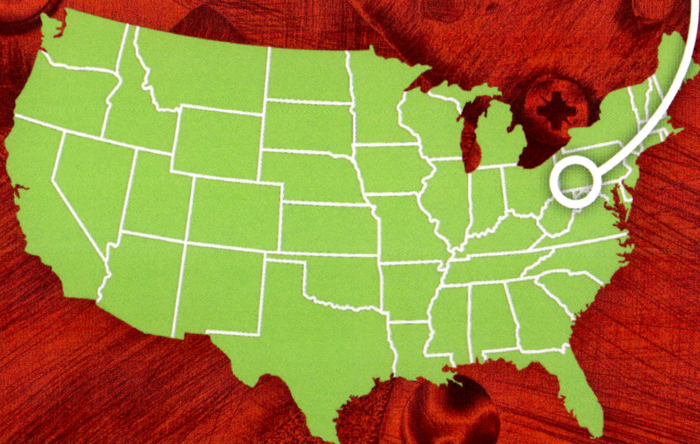

Many people work on a house. **Inspectors** check the work after each step.

Step by Step

1. An architect makes plans.

2. Workers clear land and build the foundation.

3. Carpenters build floors, walls, and a roof.

4. Workers install wires, pipes, and HVAC parts.

5. Workers paint and finish the inside.

6. The house gets a final inspection.

They make sure the house is safe.

Home

Dinner is cooking in the kitchen. There is a fort in the living room.

A family enjoys their new home!

Glossary

architect—a person who designs houses and other structures

carpenters—people who build things with wood

concrete—a hard, strong building material made with cement, sand, rocks, and water

drywall—boards made of paper and other materials that are used to finish walls

electricians—people who put in or fix wires and other electrical items in a house

faucets—parts used for controlling the flow of water from pipes

foundation—a base or support on top of which a structure is built

HVAC system—the system that warms or cools the air in a house; HVAC stands for heating, ventilation, and air conditioning.

inspectors—people who check to make sure work was done correctly

install—to set up for people to use

insulation—a material that helps keep the air inside of a house the right temperature

permits—agreements that give someone permission to build or work on a house

plumbers—people who put in or fix pipes, sinks, and other parts of a house where water flows

To Learn More

AT THE LIBRARY

Herrick, Becky. *How It's Built: House.* New York, N.Y.: Scholastic, 2022.

Manushkin, Fran. *Mr. Patel Builds.* North Mankato, Minn.: Picture Window Books, 2021.

Toolen, Avery. *A Day with a Construction Worker.* Minneapolis, Minn.: Jump!, 2022.

ON THE WEB

FACTSURFER

Factsurfer.com gives you a safe, fun way to find more information.

1. Go to www.factsurfer.com.
2. Enter "house" into the search box and click 🔍.
3. Select your book cover to see a list of related content.

Index

architect, 6
basement, 9
building permits, 7
carpenters, 10
concrete, 9
doors, 11
drywall, 16
electricians, 14, 17
Fallingwater, 17
family, 4, 21
faucets, 17
floors, 10
foundation, 8, 9
frames, 10, 16
HVAC system, 14, 15
inspectors, 18
insulation, 16
lights, 17
nail guns, 10, 11
paint, 16
parts of a house, 11
pipes, 13
plans, 6, 7
plumbers, 13, 17
roof, 10
sinks, 17
step by step, 19
walls, 10, 16
what do you need?, 9
windows, 11
wires, 14
wood, 10
workers, 4, 8, 9, 11, 14, 16

The images in this book are reproduced through the courtesy of: Pajor Pawel, cover top hero; J.D.S, cover bottom hero; Alison Hancoc, pp. 2-3; Dennis MacDonald, p. 4; Monkey Business, pp. 4-5; BalanceFormcreative, p. 6; StudioDin, p. 6 (drawing plans); Francesco Scatena, p. 7; Greg Kelton, pp. 8-9, 19 (step two); northlight, p. 8 (foundation); bybarn, p. 9 (concrete); shablovskyistock, p. 9 (wood); BillionPhotos.com, p. 9 (wires); ronstik, p. 9 (pipes); Ingus Evertovskis, p. 9 (ducts); Alekss, p. 9 (insulation); contrastwerkstatt, p. 9 (drywall); Sebastian Duda, p. 9 (paint); Studio D, pp. 10-11; Robert Kneschke, p. 10 (windows); BM_27, p. 11 (floors, house); Kelly Headrick, p. 12; ungvar, pp. 12-13, 14; 娜 赵, p. 13; Tomasz Zajda, pp. 14-15; bilanol, p. 16; Serhii, p. 16 (faucet); Sean Pavone, p. 17; Louis-Photo, pp. 18-19; Carlos E. Santa Maria, p. 19 (step one); Victor, p. 19 (step three); puhimec, p. 19 (step four); Antonio Gravante, p. 19 (step five); Brian, p. 19 (step six); Jacob Lund, pp. 20-21; PeopleImages.com - Yuri A, p. 20 (cooking); karamysh, pp. 22-23, 24 (background); Sheila Say, p. 23.